NEW MEXICO

Past and Present

Corona Brezina

rosen publishing's
rosen central®

New York

Published in 2011 by The Rosen Publishing Group, Inc.
29 East 21st Street, New York, NY 10010

Library of Congress Cataloging-in-Publication Data

Brezina, Corona.
New Mexico: past and present / Corona Brezina. — 1st ed.
    p. cm. — (The United States: past and present)
Includes bibliographical references and index.
ISBN 978-1-4358-9490-7 (library binding)
ISBN 978-1-4358-9517-1 (pbk.)
ISBN 978-1-4358-9551-5 (6-pack)
1. New Mexico—Juvenile literature. I. Title.
F796.3.B69 2010
978.9—dc22

2010003059

Manufactured in Malaysia

CPSIA Compliance Information: Batch #S10YA: For further information, contact Rosen Publishing, New York, New York, at 1-800-237-9932.

On the cover: Top left: A 1915 postcard depicts members of the Hopi Indian tribe performing the Basket Dance, an annual tradition celebrating the end of the harvest. Top right: A visitor to Carlsbad Caverns National Park passes by the Texas Toothpick, one of many spectacular rock formations found in the caves. Bottom: Hot air balloons dot the sky above the Rio Grande during the 2008 Albuquerque International Balloon Fiesta. The annual event is the world's largest balloon festival.

Contents

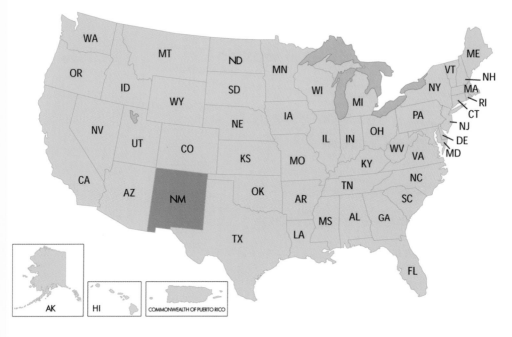

Though large in area, New Mexico has one of the lowest population densities in the nation. The population is mainly concentrated in the northern half of the state.

Introduction

Mention the state of New Mexico and people immediately summon up images of pueblo villages and scenic canyon landscapes. New Mexico is known for its sunny weather, Wild West legacy, and rich Native American and early colonial heritage. It is the state most associated with roadrunners, chili peppers, turquoise jewelry, and adobe brick. Santa Fe is the oldest state capital in the United States. The Palace of the Governors, built in Santa Fe in 1610, is the nation's oldest public building.

What draws people to New Mexico? For some, it's their ancestral heritage. The Pueblo people of modern New Mexico are descended from the Ancestral Puebloans, who built a civilization in New Mexico over a millennium ago. Some Hispanic New Mexicans also have deep roots in the state. Santa Fe was founded a decade before the pilgrims landed at Plymouth Rock.

In the nineteenth century, Americans swarmed to the Wild West in search of gold, silver, ranch land, and adventure. During World War II, scientists chose to develop the atomic bomb in an isolated area of New Mexico. Artists were drawn to the cultural as well as scenic landscape. Today, retirees come to New Mexico for the mild, dry weather, and illegal immigrants cross the border in search of the American Dream. Tourists and natives alike can still experience the broad vistas and natural wonders that have welcomed newcomers throughout the state's long history.

Chapter 1

The Geography of
NEW MEXICO

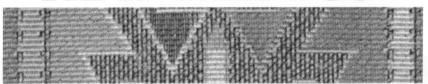

With an area of 121,356 square miles (314,310 square kilometers), New Mexico is the fifth largest state in the United States. It is located in the Southwest region of the country. It is bordered by Colorado to the north, Arizona to the west, and Oklahoma and Texas to the east. Mexico and Texas make up its southern border. New Mexico is called one of the Four Corners states because at its northeast corner, Utah, Colorado, Arizona, and New Mexico meet at a crossroads. New Mexico's largest cities are Albuquerque, Las Cruces, Rio Rancho, and Santa Fe, the state capital.

Geographic Features

New Mexico consists of four geographic regions. The northwestern corner of the state is part of the Colorado Plateau, an elevated landmass that also extends across parts of Arizona, Utah, and Colorado. Millions of years ago, flowing water eroded the Colorado Plateau to form canyons, cliffs, and rock formations such as mesas and buttes. Other rock formations, such as the monumental Shiprock, were created by the eruptions of ancient volcanoes.

The second geographic region is the Rocky Mountains. They extend into the north-central part of the state. The mountain chain

The rock formation Shiprock is sacred to the Navajo Indians, who know it as Tse Bitai, or "winged rock." Since it is a sacred site, climbing the landmark is forbidden.

to the east is called the Sangre de Cristo Mountains; New Mexico's tallest peaks are in this range. Wheeler Peak, near Taos, is the highest point in the state, at 13,167 feet (4,013 meters). Smaller mountain chains extend to the south and west.

The eastern third of the state is part of the Great Plains—the flat, grassy expanse that makes up much of the central United States. The region is scattered with occasional mesas and other rock formations. Part of the New Mexican great plains, the high plains are known as the Llano Estacado. Carlsbad Caverns, New Mexico's only national park, is located in the Great Plains region.

Carlsbad Caverns

One evening in 1898, a young cowhand named James White went to investigate an unusual plume of smoke rising in the distance. He discovered that the smoke was actually a cloud of thousands of bats flying out of the mouth of a cave. White climbed down 60 feet (18 m) into the cave on a rope ladder and entered one of the largest and most extensive systems of caverns in the world. He spent all of his free time exploring the caves by lantern, describing the underground wonders to friends who never believed his fantastical stories.

Carlsbad Caverns has its origins in a limestone reef created 250 million years ago near the shores of an inland sea. Several million years ago, the rock layer was lifted up and the reef became part of the Guadalupe Mountains. Sulfuric acid carved a network of caverns into the limestone. Later, as the uplift continued, water trickled through and decorated the rock with mineral deposits.

The cave system consists of 116 rooms meandering for more than 30 miles (50 km). Stalactites hang from the ceilings, and stalagmites reach upward from the floor. Some of the most impressive formations have been given names such as Iceberg Rock, Hall of Giants, and the Whale's Mouth. The largest cave, the Big Room, is the second largest chamber in the world. Its ceiling is 255 feet (77.7 m) high, and the floor area is as large as fourteen football fields.

In 1923, the government sent mineral examiner Robert Holley to investigate James White's reports. Holley was stunned by the natural wonders of the caves, and he recommended that the site be named a national monument. In 1930, Carlsbad Caverns was designated a national park. Today, visitors can take an elevator 750 feet (230 m) down to the Big Room and explore 3 miles (4.8 km) of the caverns. Bats still inhabit the caverns, and people gather every summer evening to watch about four hundred thousand of them emerge.

Southwestern and central New Mexico are part of the Basin and Range Province. This area is marked by mountain ranges alternating with long valleys. It includes fertile farmland as well as desert expanses. One spectacular desert area is the White Sands National Monument, nestled within the Tularosa Valley.

New Mexico's white sand dunes cover an area of 275 square miles (712 sq km), making up the largest white gypsum field in the world.

New Mexico's dominant river is the Rio Grande, which extends for 1,900 miles (3,100 km) from north to south. It enters the state from Colorado and cuts through the Rocky Mountains, at one point flowing through the deep Rio Grande Gorge. From there, it runs southward through the Basin and Range Province and forms a stretch of the border with Mexico. Other important rivers in New Mexico include the Pecos River, the Canadian River, the Chama River, the San Juan River, and the Gila River. The Continental Divide crosses New Mexico and determines which direction the rivers flow. Rivers east of the Continental Divide eventually drain into the Atlantic Ocean. Rivers west of the Continental Divide drain into the Pacific Ocean.

New Mexico contains only 234 square miles (606 sq km) of inland water. The major bodies of water in the state are man-made reservoirs created by damming rivers. New Mexico's largest lake, Elephant Butte Lake, was created in 1916 by damming the Rio Grande.

Climate

New Mexico's climate is generally warm and dry, but there is significant variation in temperature and precipitation from one region to another. Southern areas of the state can experience summer heat waves with temperatures greater than 100 degrees Fahrenheit (38 degrees Celsius). The northern part of the state sees more temperate summer weather, but average winter temperatures here can drop to 35°F (1.7°C).

Most of New Mexico receives very little precipitation, but precipitation levels vary widely from north to south. The northern mountains can receive 300 inches (762 cm) of snow during winter. Southern deserts may receive less than 1 inch (2.6 cm) of rain annually. Summer is the wettest season. Intense afternoon monsoon thunderstorms can cause dry arroyos, desert gullies, to fill with water and lead to dangerous flash floods.

Wildlife of New Mexico

New Mexico supports a rich diversity of plant and animal life. This is because New Mexico's regions and climate vary so dramatically, from the low, hot flatland of the south, to the chilly peaks of its tallest mountains.

Vegetation in southern New Mexico includes plants such as yucca, cacti, mesquite, and creosote bushes that are adapted to dry conditions. Various grasses, including blue grama—the official state grass—grow on the Great Plains. Northward, as the altitude rises, trees such as juniper, oak, and ponderosa pine dominate. New Mexico's state tree, the *piñon* pine, grows here. It is the source of pine/*piñon* nuts. Much of north-central New Mexico, especially mountainous areas, is covered by thick forests. Lower-altitude forests are made up of oak, juniper, Douglas fir, and ponderosa pine trees. During the summer, wildflowers such as columbine and New Mexico groundsel grow in woodland meadows. Higher altitude forests consist of trees such as spruces, firs, and aspens. At the highest zones, only a few forms of plant life, such as bristlecone pines and some summer wildflowers, can survive.

New Mexico's animal life also varies, depending on temperature and availability of water. The state bird, the roadrunner, lives in the desert. Other desert dwellers include rodents, scorpions, javelinas, tarantulas, various lizards

Native to New Mexico, the javelina belongs to the peccary family, a group of hoofed mammals with sharp tusks that originated in South America.

(including the endangered Gila monster), and snakes, including poisonous prairie rattlers and diamondbacks. Pronghorns are common on the Great Plains, and coyotes and mountain lions range across the state. The forests support a wide range of animals, including black bears, elk, muskrat, squirrels, marmots, bobcats, porcupines, and game birds such as quail and wild turkey. Bighorn sheep and pikas live at higher altitudes. Dozens of different species of birds live in the forests, including the spotted owl. New Mexico's streams, lakes, and rivers are home to various fish, turtles, and amphibians.

Chapter 2

THE HISTORY OF NEW MEXICO

The first inhabitants of New Mexico may have arrived as early as twenty thousand years ago on the trail of big game such as mammoth and bison. Archaeological evidence shows that twelve thousand years ago, two separate cultures hunted game across New Mexico. The Sandia were in the north and the Clovis in the south. A thousand years later, the Folsom people emerged in northeastern New Mexico.

The big-game hunters were succeeded by Native Americans who spread northward from Mexico and South America. They established permanent settlements, wove baskets, and farmed crops such as corn, squash, and beans. Around 500 CE, the Mogollon culture arose in southwestern New Mexico. They lived in pit houses dug into the ground. The Mogollon developed pottery, and one group—the Mimbres—created beautiful black-and-white designs.

To the northwest, the Ancestral Puebloans (sometimes called the Anasazi) developed a sophisticated culture beginning about 850 CE. They carved stone dwellings into the sides of cliffs and constructed pueblos, multistoried adobe houses, consisting of hundreds of rooms. The pueblos featured large underground chambers called kivas used for ceremonies. At Chaco Canyon, the largest settlement, the Ancestral Puebloans built an irrigation system for their crops.

The Mogollon and Ancestral Puebloans abandoned their homelands between 1300 and 1450, perhaps as a result of a prolonged drought. Present-day Pueblo tribes such as the Acoma, Zuñi, and Taos are thought to be descendants of the Ancestral Puebloans. Beginning around 1000 CE, Navajo and Apache groups began migrating from Canada to the Southwest. They led a nomadic existence of hunting and gathering.

Beginning about 1150, Ancestral Puebloans built cliff houses and pueblo dwellings at present-day Bandolier National Monument.

Exploration and Settlement

The first European to explore New Mexico was the Spanish Franciscan priest Marcos de Niza. He led a 1539 expedition in search of the mythical Seven Cities of Cibola, supposedly a source of great treasure. The conquistador Francisco Vásquez de Coronado followed in 1540, leading more than a thousand soldiers and Native American allies. He explored the Southwest for two years. He found no gold and began a pattern of conflict between Europeans and Pueblo natives.

In 1598, Juan de Oñate led a group of settlers, soldiers, and clergy up the Rio Grande. He founded the colony of New Mexico, which extended across most of the Southwest. He established New Mexico's

A covered wagon crosses a New Mexico creek in an 1867 photo taken by Alexander Gardner, who traveled to the West working as a photographer for a railroad survey.

first capital, a settlement called San Gabriel. After thirteen Spaniards were killed by Native Americans, Oñate responded brutally, killing thousands and enslaving and torturing many others in retaliation. The settlers and soldiers were disappointed to find no gold in the region, and many deserted. The settlement failed to take root. In 1609, Don Pedro de Peralta became governor of New Mexico and established a new capital at La Villa Real de la Santa Fé de San Francisco de Asis—Santa Fe.

Priests set up missions across New Mexico so that they could convert the Native Americans to Christianity. The Native Americans resented the forced conversions and the destruction of their traditional culture. In 1680, a Pueblo uprising drove the Spanish out of New Mexico. Twelve years later, Spanish general Diego de Vargas recaptured Santa Fe. From then on, the Spaniards showed more acceptance of Native American customs. There was relatively little conflict with Pueblo Native Americans throughout the eighteenth century. As colonists spread out across the region, however, they often clashed with tribes such as the Comanche and Apache.

In 1807, American Lieutenant Zebulon Pike and a party of men crossed into Spanish territory. Spanish soldiers arrested the men and took them to Santa Fe. The men were treated well and upon their release, Pike published an account of his journey. It sparked interest in New Mexico among Americans.

The Mexican War of Independence began in 1810, but the fighting did not reach New Mexico. In 1821, the Spanish recognized Mexico's independence, and New Mexico became part of the newly established Republic of Mexico. Americans could now travel freely across the border. This marked the beginning of the Santa Fe Trail, a route used by traders and settlers.

Territorial Days

In 1846, the United States declared war on Mexico. American general Stephen Watts Kearny and about one thousand soldiers marched along the Santa Fe Trail to Santa Fe. They met with no resistance, and Kearny took possession of New Mexico peaceably. Kearny continued on toward California, appointing Charles Bent as governor of New Mexico. Resentful of the new rule, New Mexicans killed Bent and several other officials during the Revolt of 1847. The American army quickly put down the rebellion.

The Mexican-American War ended in victory for the Americans in 1848. New Mexico became a U.S. territory in 1850. Its area increased with the Gadsden Purchase of 1853, which included the southwestern corner of present-day New Mexico. In 1863, the New Mexico Territory—a huge region—was divided, and the western half became the Arizona Territory.

In 1861, the Civil War broke out between the North and South. New Mexico remained loyal to the Union, although some residents sympathized with the Confederacy. Confederate general Henry Hopkins Sibley led a force of men to the Southwest, planning to capture

A railroad runs through the coal mining camp of Allison, a company town where employees lived in houses provided by Diamond Coal Company, seen at right.

territory for the Confederacy all the way to San Francisco. In February 1862, the Confederates won the Battle of Valverde in southern New Mexico, but they did not decisively defeat Union forces. In March, Union troops prevailed at the Battle of Glorieta Pass in northern New Mexico. The Confederates were forced to retreat from the territory.

Conflict with Native Americans continued, and the military moved aggressively to subdue them. In 1864, Kit Carson drove the Navajo from their lands by burning their crops and killing their livestock. He sent eight thousand Native Americans on the grueling 300-mile (500 km) Long Walk, on which hundreds died, to remote Bosque Redondo. There, more than two thousand died of smallpox and starvation. In 1868, they were allowed to resettle in the newly established Navajo reservation. Meanwhile, the Apache chief Cochise, succeeded by Geronimo, led a rebellion that ended when Geronimo surrendered in 1886.

After the Civil War ended, settlers swarmed to New Mexico. As railroads reached New Mexico in the 1870s and 1880s, the journey to the Southwest became easier than ever before. Ranchers arrived with huge herds of cattle and sheep, farmers began irrigating crops, and miners came with hopes of making their fortunes. Mining boomtowns could spring up overnight, then fade into ghost towns when people moved on. Disagreements were too often decided with guns as New Mexicans took the law into their own hands. Stories of the Wild West tell of outlaws, cattle rustlers, train robbers, cowboys, and sheriffs. The town of Cimarron, in particular, was well known for its rowdy ways.

Statehood and Growth

In 1910, New Mexican delegates met for a constitutional convention, the first step toward New Mexico becoming a U.S. state. Voters

Billy the Kid

Billy the Kid (Henry McCarty, aka Bill Bonney), who once claimed to have killed twenty-one people by the age of twenty-one, is the most legendary outlaw of the Wild West. Born around 1860, Billy the Kid had his first brush with the law in 1875, when he was arrested for a prank at a Chinese laundry in Silver City. He escaped from jail and wandered around New Mexico working as a cattle hand. In 1877, he killed a man playing cards and fled the scene.

Soon afterward, Billy wound up in the Lincoln County War, the bloodiest range war of the Old West. The conflict began as a power struggle between the owners of L. G. Murphy and Co., the only general store in Lincoln County, and lawyer Alexander McSween and wealthy cattleman John Chisum. Billy became involved when he agreed to work for cattleman John Tunstall, an ally of Chisum's. When a group of sheriff's deputies shot and killed Tunstall, it sent Billy on a vendetta. He joined a posse called the Regulators, and they hunted down Tunstall's killers. The Lincoln County War ended with a five-day battle in the center of Lincoln, but victory went to the politically well-connected owners of the general store. A force of gunfighters surrounded McSween and the Regulators inside his house and burned it down, killing McSween and many others.

Billy escaped and took up cattle rustling as a fugitive, but he was intrigued when Governor Lew Wallace offered amnesty to some participants in the Lincoln County War. He negotiated by letter with the governor and met with him directly. In 1880, Sheriff Pat Garrett, a former friend of Billy's, arrested him. He was put on trial and sentenced to hang. Billy escaped, killing two deputies.

Billy didn't go far, though. In July 1881, Garrett caught up with him at Fort Sumner and killed him.

Today, Billy the Kid has inspired artists like author Gore Vidal and filmmaker Sam Peckinpah to create books, movies, and TV specials about his life. Fort Sumner has a Billy the Kid Museum. New Mexico's Web site offers a Billy the Kid travel itinerary, and historic sites related to Billy have been preserved.

approved the constitution in 1911. President William Taft formally admitted New Mexico as the forty-seventh state in 1912. William C. McDonald became the first governor of the new state.

Soon afterward, World War I broke out in Europe. New Mexico was also affected by the revolution across the border in Mexico. In 1916, the rebel leader Pancho Villa and a band of revolutionaries raided a military base at Columbus, New Mexico, killing eighteen people. U.S. troops pursued Villa into Mexico but withdrew without confronting him.

During the Great Depression, which lasted from 1929 to 1934, New Mexicans, like all Americans, suffered. Many people lost their jobs and even their homes. Some were helped by the New Deal, which put New Mexicans to work on projects such as building roads and state park facilities.

More than sixty-five thousand New Mexicans served in the U.S. Army during World War II, which lasted from 1939 to 1945. Two New Mexican regiments endured the horrifying Bataan Death March in the Philippines. Many soldiers died on the march or later in prison camps. Other New Mexicans, the Navajo and Apache "code talkers," used their native languages to transmit messages and keep information out of enemy hands. Back at home, the government established military installations in New Mexico. The most important project, the top-secret Manhattan Project, led to the development of the atomic bomb.

From 1940 to 1980, the population of New Mexico tripled, and it has continued to rise steadily. Although the state has the sixth-lowest population density in the nation, New Mexicans have become increasingly urbanized. New Mexico has the largest proportion of Hispanics of any state. Its Native American and Hispanic populations contribute to the state's rich cultural heritage.

Chapter 3

THE GOVERNMENT OF NEW MEXICO

As is the case in every state, New Mexico is governed at the local, state, and federal levels. Counties and municipalities have local governments. There are thirty-three counties in New Mexico. Each is governed by a three-to-five-member board of commissioners elected to two-year terms. Voters also elect a clerk, treasurer, assessor, sheriff, and probate judge for each county. The largest county in New Mexico is Bernalillo County, where Albuquerque is the county seat. Municipalities—which include cities, towns, and villages—also have their own governments, as do school districts and special districts.

Native American tribes in New Mexico administer their own affairs through tribal governments. There are nineteen Pueblo groups in New Mexico. Each governs its own community through tribal councils. In addition, the Pueblo participate in the All-Indian Pueblo Council, a coalition system. The Navajo Nation, the largest tribe in the United States, is spread across three states, including New Mexico. The capital of the Navajo Nation is in Window Rock, Arizona. The Navajo Nation is governed by a council of eighty-eight elected members. There is also an executive branch headed by an elected president. Two Apache tribes, the Jicarilla and the Mescalero, each govern through a tribal council. In New Mexico's state government, the

Indian Affairs Department is a cabinet-level department that works alongside tribal governments.

Branches of State Government

State government in New Mexico is centered in Santa Fe, the oldest capital city in the United States. The New Mexico Legislature meets in the state capitol, sometimes

Leaders of the All-Indian Pueblo Council are shown after being sworn in to office in 2007 at Santo Domingo Pueblo.

called the Roundhouse. Dedicated in 1966, it is one of the newest capitol buildings in the United States. It is the only round state capitol. Elements of its design are based on Pueblo architecture and Native American motifs—the building's shape resembles a Zia sun symbol, which is also featured on the state flag.

New Mexico is governed under the state constitution adopted in 1911, with some amendments. The state government is organized into executive, legislative, and judicial branches.

The executive branch is headed by a governor. Other elected officials in the executive branch include the lieutenant governor, who is elected jointly with the governor, as well as a secretary of state, a state treasurer, an attorney general, a commissioner of public lands, and five public regulation commissioners. Officials can only serve two consecutive terms of four years.

21

Los Alamos

In 1942, top scientists from across the country began arriving at a former boys' school on the remote Los Alamos Ranch. The site was one of the research labs for the Manhattan Project, the top-secret effort to develop an atomic bomb. Physicist J. Robert Oppenheimer was appointed scientific director and General Leslie R. Groves served as the military officer in charge of the project. Because of the secrecy, many newcomers did not even know their destination. Mail was sent to a post office box in Santa Fe. Makeshift housing was erected for researchers and their families, and trainloads of sophisticated scientific equipment arrived. Los Alamos quickly became a modern-day boomtown. By the end of World War II, the site had grown into a town of six thousand people.

The scientists and engineers worked long days for two years. Although there were many sites involved in the Manhattan Project, Los Alamos was the primary laboratory for theoretical and experimental research. It was also the site for the final assembly of nuclear weapons. On July 16, 1945, the first atomic bomb was tested. Called the Trinity test, it was carried out in the desert near Alamogordo, 240 miles (386 km) south of Los Alamos. Light from the blast was visible for hundreds of miles, and the impact knocked down an observer 5 miles (8 km) away from the explosion. Two weeks later, the military dropped atomic bombs on two cities in Japan.

After World War II, nuclear research continued at the Los Alamos National Laboratory. One of the original divisions of the Manhattan Project was transformed into the Sandia National Laboratory. The focus of Los Alamos National Laboratory has shifted from development and testing to stewardship of the nation's stockpile of nuclear weapons. When the Cold War ended, the lab broadened its focus to address issues related to energy, environment, infrastructure, health, and global security. During the early 2000s, there were a number of high-profile security lapses at the lab.

In 2006, Democrat Bill Richardson won reelection to a second term as governor. Richardson began his political career in the U.S. House of Representatives, where he served as a representative from 1983 to 1997. Before he was elected New Mexico's governor, Richardson served as U.S. ambassador to the United Nations and then as energy secretary in the administration of Bill Clinton. In 2008,

New Mexico's state legislature meets in the lower level of the Roundhouse. The capitol building also houses a collection of works by New Mexican artists.

Richardson campaigned for the Democratic presidential nomination but dropped out early in the primary process.

The state legislature—the branch of government that makes laws—is divided into two houses: a forty-two-member senate and a seventy-member house of representatives. Senators hold office for four-year terms, and representatives are elected to two-year terms. Legislators in New Mexico are unpaid, except for a gas mileage reimbursement and a per diem allowance. Most of the year, they work at jobs outside of the government. Legislators meet for sixty days out of every odd-numbered year and for thirty days out of every even-numbered year, as well as for special sessions.

The highest court in New Mexico is the state supreme court. It consists of five justices who serve eight-year terms. The next highest court, the court of appeals, is made up of ten judges who also serve eight-year terms. New Mexico's counties are organized into thirteen

New Mexico's Supreme Court Building was built in 1937. It was a Public Works Administration (PWA) project intended to give people jobs during the Great Depression.

judicial districts. There are eighty-three district judges who are elected to six-year terms. Lesser courts include metropolitan courts, municipal courts, and magistrate courts. In addition, each county is served by a probate judge. All judges in New Mexico are elected to office.

National Representation

New Mexico sends two senators to the U.S. Senate, where they serve six-year terms. Democrat Jeff Bingaman was reelected to his fifth term of office in 2006. Before being elected to the Senate, Bingaman served in the U.S. Army Reserve from 1968 to 1974 and was elected attorney general of New Mexico in 1978. Democrat Tom Udall took office in 2009. Before becoming a senator, he was attorney general of New Mexico from 1991 to 1999 and served five terms in the U.S. House of Representatives.

New Mexico sends three representatives, one from each of three districts, to the U.S. House of Representatives, where they serve two-year terms. In 2008, New Mexicans elected three Democratic representatives to office.

In presidential elections, New Mexico tends to be a swing state. New Mexicans have voted for Democratic candidates in thirteen elections and Republican candidates in twelve elections since New Mexico became a state in 1912. In the 2008 presidential election, Barack Obama won by a wide margin.

Chapter 4

THE ECONOMY OF NEW MEXICO

A thousand years ago, the Ancestral Puebloans farmed and traded goods such as silver and turquoise jewelry. Spanish colonists also grew crops, and they established cattle and sheep ranches. In the nineteenth century, miners arrived in search of gold, silver, and other minerals.

Agriculture and mining still contribute to New Mexico's economy, but these sectors have been overshadowed by modern economic forces. Today, New Mexicans work at jobs developing high-tech products. They welcome tourists to the many scenic and historical attractions in the state. New Mexicans continue to look toward the future: In 2009, construction began on Spaceport America, the first space tourism launchpad.

Agriculture

Less than 4 percent of New Mexicans are employed in agriculture, but 60 percent of the state's area is farmland. About 90 percent of this is pasture ground for livestock. Dairy cows and beef cattle generate the most revenue of any agricultural sector. Other livestock raised in New Mexico include sheep and hogs.

New Mexico is the nation's leading producer of chile peppers. There are numerous varieties of New Mexico chiles, many developed at New Mexico State University's Chile Breeding and Genetics Program.

Irrigation makes farming possible in some of the drier areas of the state. New Mexico's major crops include hay, tree nuts such as pecans, sorghum, wheat, cotton, peanuts, and vegetables. Chile peppers, a staple in New Mexican cooking, are an important crop.

Mining and Forestry

New Mexico's most important mineral resources are fossil fuels—coal, oil, and natural gas. The state is also the third largest copper producer in the country. The Chino open-pit mine is New Mexico's

The Santa Fe Trail

In 1821, a Missouri trader named William Bucknell led a small group of traders westward to trade goods with Native Americans. The band encountered a group of Mexican soldiers. Bucknell feared that he would be penalized for crossing into Mexico illegally. Instead, the soldiers urged him to continue on to Santa Fe. There, Bucknell sold his goods and returned laden with silver. The next year, he organized a much larger expedition to Santa Fe. Over the next six decades, many other travelers followed his route.

The Santa Fe Trail was the international commercial highway of its day, and it was vital to American expansion into the southwestern territories during the nineteenth century. The 900-mile (1,450 km) route ran from Missouri to New Mexico, passing through five states. Teams of oxen pulled wagons that could be loaded with more than 2 tons (1.81 metric tons) of goods. Traders traveled in caravans of about one hundred wagons. Travelers could take the main arm of the trail that arced north through Colorado—the Mountain Branch—or they could opt for the slightly shorter route—the Cimarron Cutoff—that passed through the desert. They faced hazards such as rattlesnake bites, attacks by hostile Native Americans, water shortages, and violent prairie thunderstorms.

After New Mexico became an American territory, the army erected forts to protect the Santa Fe Trail from Native American attacks. Miners, settlers, trappers, and adventurers joined traders and soldiers on the route. Stagecoach companies ran lines along the Santa Fe Trail. At its peak in the 1860s, five thousand wagons a year would make the eight-week journey to Santa Fe.

The arrival of railways in the 1880s ended the era of the Santa Fe Trail. In 1987, it was declared a National Historic Trail by Congress. In some places, wagon ruts in the prairie mark the route of the Santa Fe Trail to this day.

oldest active copper mine. It is also one of the largest in the world. New Mexico is the nation's leading producer of potash, which is used in making products such as soap and fertilizer. Other minerals produced in New Mexico include gold, silver, gypsum, iron ore, lead, lime, mica, molybdenum, perlite, pumice, and tungsten. Crushed stone, sand, and gravel are also mined for construction. The state also possesses uranium deposits, especially on the Navajo reservation. Although most uranium mining in the state ceased in the 1980s, in February 2009, the state's house of representatives passed a bill to examine renewing uranium mining.

In the northern forests, timber companies cut trees and process them into lumber. The ponderosa pine is the primary tree harvested.

Federal Jobs

The presence of military installations and national laboratories has contributed to a long history of technological innovation in New Mexico. It has also promoted the development of a highly educated workforce. According to the office of the governor, New Mexico has more people with Ph.D. degrees per capita than any other state. Federal spending is an important driver of New Mexico's economy.

The Very Large Array studies galactic marvels from nebulae to black holes. It consists of twenty-seven radio antennae 82 feet (25 m) in diameter.

Shoppers check out a handcrafted chest during the Traditional Spanish Market, an annual Santa Fe event. The market also features live music, dancing, and regional foods.

There are three air force bases, a missile testing range, army facilities, and three research laboratories in the state. The government also operates the Very Large Array, a radio astronomy observatory, in New Mexico. Much of the government research focuses on space exploration and rocket development.

Industry and Technology

High-tech industries have become a major force in New Mexico's economy, partly as a result of government activities in New Mexico. Private companies sometimes develop scientific breakthroughs made in government labs. Manufacturers also supply parts and instruments to government facilities.

Important manufactured products include electronic equipment, transportation and aviation equipment, and instruments such as navigational devices. Used in computers and electronic gear, semiconductor chips are an important industry in New Mexico, and the semiconductor giant Intel is a major employer. The solar energy industry has been expanding in New Mexico as well.

Service Sector and Tourism

The service sector accounts for the biggest share of New Mexico's economy. The sector encompasses financial businesses (such as real estate and insurance); retail, hospitality, and leisure (such as restaurants and hotels); and professional services (such as accountants). The government, which provides a range of service jobs, is the state's biggest employer.

The tourism industry is an important contributor to the state's economy as well. New Mexico offers attractions that appeal to a wide variety of people. One particularly popular event is the Albuquerque International Balloon Fiesta, a nine-day hot-air balloon festival held every year in Albuquerque. It is the largest hot-air balloon event in the world, attracting up to one hundred thousand spectators a day. There are also many Native American and Spanish colonial sites that represent the state's cultural and historic heritage. Nature lovers can explore scenic parks and monuments, while more active visitors can go skiing, hiking, and camping. New Mexico is well known for its art and artists, and there are many galleries, museums, art fairs, and studios in small towns as well as in the larger cities. In Roswell, the International UFO Museum and Research Center focuses on the UFO crash of 1947. (The U.S. military maintains that the wreckage was an experimental weather balloon, not a flying saucer, and that no alien corpses were recovered.)

Chapter 5

PEOPLE FROM NEW MEXICO:
PAST AND PRESENT

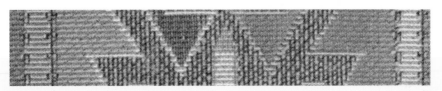

During its long history as a colony and a state, New Mexico has produced many notable figures, especially in the arts.

John Denver (1943–1997) Born in Roswell, John Denver became popular in the 1970s as a folk/pop singer and songwriter. His hit songs include "Rocky Mountain High" and "Take Me Home, Country Roads," and fifteen of his albums reached the Top 40 charts.

Pete Domenici (1932–) Republican politician Pete Domenici was New Mexico's longest-serving senator. He served six terms in Congress, from 1973 to 2009. An advocate for nuclear energy, Domenici wrote a book on the subject in 2004.

Bill Gates (1955–) Bill Gates cofounded the computer software company Microsoft, and the first "Micro-soft" office was located in Albuquerque. Products such as the Windows operating system, along with Gates's shrewd business sense, turned Microsoft into one of the world's most successful

New Mexicans in the Arts and Entertainment

New Mexico has a rich artistic heritage. Native Americans do traditional crafts such as pottery, woodcarving, and weaving. Artists have flocked to the art colony at Taos for more than a century. Santa Fe has a thriving arts scene, and it is known for its performing arts as well as its support of artists and folk artists.

R. C. Gorman (1931–2005) was a Navajo artist who lived and owned a gallery in Taos. He is best known for his paintings of Native American women, though he also sculpted and made lithographs. Peter Hurd (1904–1984), whose family owned a ranch near Roswell, painted many New Mexico landscapes as well as portraits. The artist most associated with the Southwest is Georgia O'Keeffe (1887–1986), who lived and worked in New Mexico for many years. O'Keeffe painted large-scale works featuring natural objects, like flowers, and southwestern themes and landscapes. She is considered one of the greatest American artists.

New Mexico has also produced many talented figures in film and television. William Hanna (1910–2001) worked with Joseph Barbera at MGM Studios to produce the Tom and Jerry cartoons. They went on to found the Hanna-Barbera animation studio, which produced *The Flintstones*, *The Jetsons*, *Scooby-Doo*, and *The Smurfs*. Neil Patrick Harris (1973–), who grew up in Albuquerque, has acted in theater, film, and television. He is known for *Doogie Howser, M.D.*, *Starship Troopers*, the *Harold and Kumar* films, and *How I Met Your Mother*. Actress Demi Moore (1962–), who was born in Roswell, starred in a number of highly success-ful movies including *Ghost*, *A Few Good Men*, and *Charlie's Angels: Full Throttle*. Kim Stanley (1925–2001) was an Emmy-winning theater and film actress. She was twice nominated for both Oscar and Tony awards.

corporations and Gates into one of the world's richest men. In 2000, he and his wife established the Bill and Melinda Gates Foundation.

Robert Goddard (1882–1945) Physicist Robert Goddard was one of the pioneers in developing rockets. He launched the first liquid-fuel rocket and developed many important theories of rocketry. Goddard tested many of his rockets in New Mexico.

A former teacher and school principal, Octaviano Larrazolo supported educational opportunities for Hispanic Americans and championed civil rights.

Tony Hillerman (1925–2008) Tony Hillerman was a best-selling author known for his Navajo tribal police mystery novels. The second book in the series, *Dance Hall of the Dead*, won the prestigious Edgar Award for mysteries. Hillerman also taught journalism at the University of New Mexico for many years.

Octaviano Larrazolo (1859–1930) Octaviano Larrazolo became the fourth elected governor of New Mexico in 1918

While serving in the U.S. Army during World War II, cartoonist Bill Mauldin created a scruffy pair of soldiers named Willie and Joe for the military newspaper *Stars and Stripes*.

and the state's second Hispanic governor. He served in New Mexico's house of representatives during the 1920s. In 1928, he was elected to the U.S. Senate, becoming the first Hispanic senator. He was forced to step down after a few months due to illness.

Nancy Lopez (1957–) Professional golfer Nancy Lopez began her career at age twelve, when she won the New Mexico Women's Amateur. She went on to become the greatest female golfer of her generation, winning forty-eight Ladies Professional Golf Association (LPGA) tour events, including three championships. She was inducted into the LPGA Hall of Fame at the age of thirty.

Bill Mauldin (1921–2003) New Mexico native Bill Mauldin was a cartoonist who twice won the Pulitzer Prize. Mauldin is best remembered for his cartoons published while he was serving in the military during World War II. His cartoons depicted the everyday life of soldiers in the field.

Clyde Tombaugh (1906–1997) Astronomer Clyde Tombaugh discovered the dwarf planet Pluto in 1930. He also discovered new asteroids, star clusters, and clusters of galaxies. Tombaugh taught astronomy at New Mexico State University for many years.

Victorio (c. 1825–1880) Victorio was the chief of the Chiricahua group of Apache. In the late 1870s, after a decade of cruel treatment of his people by the U.S. government,

Award-winning journalist Linda Wertheimer was the first woman to anchor network coverage of a presidential election night—Jimmy Carter's 1976 victory over Gerald Ford.

Victorio began leading raids against soldiers and settlers. He was killed in Mexico during a two-day battle with the Mexican army.

Linda Wertheimer (1943–) Born in Carlsbad, Linda Wertheimer is a highly respected radio journalist. She served as director of the National Public Radio news show *All Things Considered* from its debut in 1971. She later served as correspondent and host.

Timeline

25000 BCE	First evidence of human habitation in New Mexico.
500 CE	The Mogollon culture emerges.
850	The Ancestral Puebloans begin constructing pueblos.
1400	The Navajo and Apache begin migrating to the Southwest.
1539	Marcos de Niza is the first European to enter what is present-day New Mexico.
1540	Francisco Vásquez de Coronado begins exploration.
1598	Juan de Oñate founds New Mexico.
1610	Santa Fe becomes the capital of New Mexico.
1680	Spaniards are driven from the Southwest by the Pueblo Revolt.
1692	Diego de Vargas recaptures Santa Fe.
1807	Zebulon Pike leads an expedition into New Mexico.
1821	Mexico gains independence and takes possession of present-day New Mexico; the Santa Fe Trail becomes an important trade route.
1850	The New Mexico Territory is established.
1853	The United States signs the Gadsden Purchase with Mexico.
1862	The Battles of Valverde and Glorieta Pass are fought; the Confederates retreat.
1864	Kit Carson defeats the Navajo and sends them on the Long Walk.
1886	Geronimo surrenders, ending the "Indian Wars."
1912	New Mexico becomes the forty-seventh U.S. state.
1916	Pancho Villa raids Columbus.
1930	Carlsbad Caverns becomes a national park.
1945	The first atomic bomb is detonated over the New Mexican desert.
1999	The Waste Isolation Pilot Plant, a nuclear waste storage site, opens.
2009	Construction begins on Spaceport America.

New Mexico at a Glance

State motto:	*Crescit eundo* ("It grows as it grows")
State capital:	Santa Fe
State flower:	Yucca
State bird:	Greater roadrunner
State tree:	Piñon pine
Statehood date and number:	January 6, 1912; forty-seventh state
State nickname:	Land of Enchantment
Total area and U.S. rank:	121,356 sq miles (314,310 sq km); fifth largest state
Population:	1,984,356
Highest elevation:	Wheeler Peak, at 13,167 ft (4,013.3 m)
Lowest elevation:	Red Bluff Reservoir, at 2,842 ft (866 m)
Major rivers:	Rio Grande, Pecos River, Canadian River, Chama River, San Juan River, Gila River

State flag

State seal

Major lakes:	Elephant Butte Lake, Navajo Lake, Conchas Lake
Hottest recorded temperature:	122°F (50°C) on June 27, 1994, at Waste Isolation Pilot Plant
Coldest recorded temperature:	-50°F (-46°C) on February 1, 1951, at Gavilan
Origin of state name:	English translation of the original Spanish name Nuevo Mexico. "Mexico" was an Aztec word meaning "place of Mexitli," an Aztec god
Chief agricultural products:	Dairy cattle, beef cattle, sheep, hogs, hay, tree nuts, grains, cotton, peanuts, vegetables
Major industries:	Electronics and computer products, transportation equipment, electrical equipment, oil refinement

Greater roadrunner

Yucca

adobe A type of clay used as a building material.

arid Very dry.

arroyo A deep gully that is usually dry, except after heavy rains.

butte An isolated mountain or hill with sloping sides and a flat top that rises abruptly above the surrounding area.

canyon A long, deep, narrow valley with steep cliff walls, often formed by running water and having a river or stream at the bottom.

caravan A group of people traveling together, often for safety when passing through a desert or hostile territory.

constitution The system of fundamental laws and principles that prescribes the nature, functions, and limits of a government or other institution.

drought A long period of abnormally low rainfall, especially one that adversely affects growing or living conditions.

gorge A narrow ravine, especially one through which a stream or river runs.

javelina A type of small wild hog.

kiva A large chamber in a Pueblo village, often underground or partly underground, used for ceremonies or councils.

mesa An isolated land formation, larger in area than a butte, with steep walls and a flat top.

plateau An area of relatively flat, elevated ground.

precipitation Any form of water that falls to the earth's surface, such as rain or snow.

pueblo A communal village or community of ancient or modern peoples in the Southwest; also, a Native American member of a pueblo.

reservation A federally owned tract of land managed by a Native American tribe.

FOR MORE INFORMATION

Carlsbad Caverns National Park

3225 National Parks Highway

Carlsbad, NM 88220

(575) 785-2232

Web site: http://www.nps.gov/cave

Visitors can find a variety of information for planning a trip to Carlsbad Caverns by accessing the National Parks Service Web site.

Museum of Indian Arts and Culture

Laboratory of Anthropology

Museum Hill, Camino Lejo, off Old Santa Fe Trail

P.O. Box 2087

Santa Fe, NM 87504

(505) 476-1269

Web site: http://www.miaclab.org

The Museum of Indian Arts and Culture hosts one of the world's most extensive collections of Native American pottery, jewelry, basketry, and weaving.

Navajo Nation

P.O. Box 9000

Window Rock, AZ 86515

(928) 871-6000

Web site: http://www.navajo.org

News, events, history, and government can be found at the official Web site of the Navajo Nation.

New Mexico Magazine

P.O. Box 12002

Santa Fe, NM 87504

(800) 898-6639

Web site: http://www.nmmagazine.com

This is the official state magazine of New Mexico.

New Mexico Museum of Art

107 West Palace Avenue

Santa Fe, NM 87501

(505) 476-5072

Web site: http://www.nmartmuseum.org

The state's oldest art museum focuses on artists of the southwest.

New Mexico Tourism Department

491 Old Santa Fe Trail

Santa Fe, NM 87501

(505) 827-7400

Web site: http://www.newmexico.org

New Mexico's official tourist site offers practical and educational information on the state.

Web Sites

Due to the changing nature of Internet links, Rosen Publishing has developed an online list of Web sites related to the subject of this book. This site is updated regularly. Please use this link to access the list:

http://www.rosenlinks.com/uspp/nmpp

FOR FURTHER READING

Anaya, Rudolfo. *ChupaCabra and the Roswell UFO*. Albuquerque, NM: University of New Mexico Press, 2008.

Blume, Judy. *Tiger Eyes*. New York, NY: Random House Children's Books, 2005.

Burgan, Michael. *New Mexico*. New York, NY: Scholastic, 2008.

Casey, Clyde. *Red or Green: New Mexico Cuisine*. Santa Fe, NM: Clear Light Books, 2007.

Elish, Dan. *The Manhattan Project*. New York, NY: Children's Press, 2007.

Ernst, Kathleen. *Secrets in the Hills: A Josefina Mystery*. Middleton, WI: Pleasant, 2006.

Glassman, Stephen. *It Happened on the Santa Fe Trail*. Guildford, CT: TwoDot, 2008.

Gómez, Arthur. *New Mexico: Images of a Land and Its People*. Albuquerque, NM: University of New Mexico Press, 2004.

Holm, Tom. *Code Talkers and Warriors: Native Americans and World War II*. New York, NY: Chelsea House, 2007.

Klages, Ellen. *The Green Glass Sea*. New York, NY: Viking, 2006.

Marriott, Barbara. *Outlaw Tales of New Mexico: True Stories of New Mexico's Most Famous Robbers, Rustlers, and Bandits*. Guildford, CT: TwoDot, 2007.

Roberts, Calvin, et al. *A History of New Mexico*. Albuquerque, NM: University of New Mexico Press, 2004.

Taschek, Karen. *Horse of Seven Moons*. Albuquerque, NM: University of New Mexico Press, 2005.

Time-Life Books. *The Gunfighters*. New York, NY: Time, Inc., 1974.

Utley, Robert M., ed. *The Story of the West: A History of the American West and Its People*. New York, NY: DK Publishing, Inc., 2003.

BIBLIOGRAPHY

Armstrong, Ruth W. *New Mexico: From Arrowhead to Atom*. 2nd ed. New York, NY: A. S. Barnes and Company, 1976.

Connell, Michelle, and Silvia Moreno. "Victorio Fought to the Death for Homeland." Borderlands, 2003–2004. Retrieved November 19, 2009 (http://dnn.epcc.edu/ nwlibrary/borderlands/22_victorio.htm).

Dary, David. *The Santa Fe Trail: Its History, Legends, and Lore*. New York, NY: Alfred A. Knopf, 2001.

DesertUSA. "Cochise, Geronimo, and Mangas Coloradas." DesertUSA.com, February 1998. Retrieved November 19, 2009 (http://www.desertusa.com/magfeb98/feb_ pap/du_apache.html).

Harbert, Nancy. *Compass American Guides: New Mexico*. 5th ed. New York, NY: Fodors LLC, 2004.

Metz, Leon Claire. *The Shooters: A Gallery of Notorious Gunmen from the American West*. New York, NY: Berkley Books, 1996.

Metzger, Stephen. *New Mexico*. 6th ed. Emeryville, CA: Avalon Travel Publishing, Inc., 2003.

New Mexico Office of the Governor. "History, Economics, Culture." 2004. Retrieved November 19, 2009 (http://www.governor.state.nm.us/history.php).

New Mexico Secretary of State. *New Mexico Blue Book 2007–2008*. 2007. Retrieved November 19, 2009 (http://www.sos.state.nm.us/sos-bluebook.html).

Sinclair, John L. *New Mexico: The Shining Land*. Albuquerque, NM: University of New Mexico Press, 1980.

Smithsonian Guide to Historic America: The Desert States. New York, NY: Stewart, Tabori & Chang, 1990.

Torrez, Robert J. "Truly an Enchanted Land." *A Cuarto Centennial History of New Mexico*. Albuquerque, NM: New Mexico Genealogical Society, 1998. Retrieved November 19, 2009 (http://www.nmgs.org/artcuarto.htm).

Utley, Robert M. *Billy the Kid: A Short and Violent Life*. Lincoln, NE: University of Nebraska Press, 1991.

Walker, Dale L. *The Calamity Papers: Western Myths and Cold Cases*. New York, NY: A Tom Doherty Associates Book, 2004.

Wiewandt, Thomas, and Maureen Wilks. *The Southwest–Inside Out: An Illustrated Guide to the Land and Its History*. 2nd ed. Tucson, AZ: Wild Horizons Publishing, 2004.

About the Author

Corona Brezina has written more than a dozen titles for Rosen Publishing. Several of her previous books have also focused on topics related to American history, including *Sojourner Truth's "Ain't I a Woman" Speech* and *The United States Past and Present: Arizona*. She lives in Chicago.

Photo Credits

Designer: Les Kanturek; Editor: Karolena Bielecki;
Photo researcher: Amy Feinberg